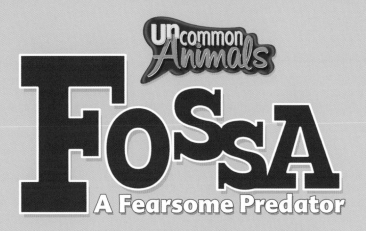

UnCommon Animals

FOSSA
A Fearsome Predator

by Meish Goldish

Consultant: Dr. Luke Dollar
Conservation Scientist
National Geographic Emerging Explorer

BEARPORT
PUBLISHING

New York, New York

Credits

Cover and Title Page, © Mark Bowler/Alamy; TOC, © Pete Oxford/Nature Picture Library; 4, © TUNS/Peter Arnold Inc.; 5, Courtesy of Luke Dollar; 6, © Chris Hellier/Corbis; 7, Courtesy of Luke Dollar; 9, © Frans Lanting/Corbis; 10, Courtesy of Luke Dollar; 11, © Huguet Pierre/BIOS/Peter Arnold Inc.; 12, © David Braun/National Geographic; 13, © Courtesy of Luke Dollar; 14T, © Pete Oxford/Nature Picture Library; 14B, © Terry Whittaker/Alamy; 15L, © Pete Oxford/Nature Picture Library; 15R, © Frans Lanting/Minden Pictures; 16, © Pete Oxford/Nature Picture Library; 17T, © Boris Liuc, Courtesy of Luke Dollar; 17B, Courtesy of Luke Dollar; 18, Courtesy of Luke Dollar; 19, Courtesy of Earthwatch; 20, © Pete Oxford/Nature Picture Library; 21, © Frans Lanting/Minden Pictures; 22, © Frans Lanting/Minden Pictures; 23, Courtesy of Luke Dollar; 24, Courtesy of Luke Dollar; 25, © Pete Oxford/Nature Picture Library; 26, © Boris Liuc, Courtesy of Luke Dollar; 27L, © Michael Melford/Stone/Getty Images; 27R, © Huguet Pierre/BIOS/Peter Arnold Inc.; 28, © Chris Hellier/Corbis; 29T, © David Haring/Oxford Scientific Films/Photolibrary; 29B, © Mark Moffett/ Minden Pictures; 32, © Pete Oxford/Nature Picture Library.

Publisher: Kenn Goin
Editorial Director: Adam Siegel
Creative Director: Spencer Brinker
Design: Dawn Beard Creative
Photo Researcher: James O'Connor

Library of Congress Cataloging-in-Publication Data

Goldish, Meish.
  Fossa : a fearsome predator / by Meish Goldish.
      p. cm. — (Uncommon animals)
  Includes bibliographical references and index.
  ISBN-13: 978-1-59716-732-1 (library binding)
  ISBN-10: 1-59716-732-0 (library binding)
  1. Fossa (Mammals)—Juvenile literature. I. Title.

  QL737.C28G65 2009
  599.74'2—dc22

                          2008004817

For more information, write to Bearport Publishing Company, Inc., 101 Fifth Avenue, Suite 6R, New York, New York 10003. Printed in the United States of America in North Mankato, Minnesota.

082010
080910CGC

10 9 8 7 6 5 4

Contents

A Murder Mystery

Deep in a forest in Madagascar, Luke Dollar was studying **rare** animals called **lemurs**. He was using **radio collars** to track their movements.

One day, Luke heard a sound that amazed him. It came from a collar that had stopped working almost eight years ago when the battery wires came loose. Now, in 1994, the collar was suddenly working again. Luke had to find out why.

Lemurs are members of a group of animals called primates. Apes, monkeys, and humans are also part of this group.

In order to track an animal in the wild, scientists sometimes place a radio collar around its neck. The collar sends out signals that scientists can follow.

Luke followed the radio signal. It led him to the lemur's collar, which had been shredded. A **predator** had chewed the collar so hard that it had pressed the wires together and started the signal again. All that was left of the lemur was a clump of fur and a few bones. What **vicious** killer could have done this?

Luke Dollar was an American college student when he came to Madagascar in 1994 to study lemurs.

A Secret Killer

Luke's guides in Madagascar could tell immediately what had killed the lemur. "Fossa (FOO-sah)!" they whispered in frightened voices.

Luke was puzzled. He was a college student who had studied many animals. Yet he had never heard of a fossa. He was curious about this mysterious creature.

The fossa is the largest predator in Madagascar.

Luke returned home to the United States. He wanted to learn more about fossas. To his surprise, he found little information about them. This only made him even more curious, however.

Luke decided to devote his studies to fossas. He knew that they lived only on the African **island** of Madagascar. So in 1996, he made the first of many trips there to study the rare animal.

Luke Dollar in Madagascar

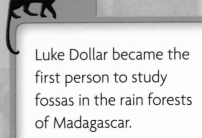

Luke Dollar became the first person to study fossas in the rain forests of Madagascar.

Welcome to Madagascar

Madagascar is a very special place. More than 200,000 different kinds of animals and plants live on the island. Many of them, including fossas and some kinds of lemurs, are found nowhere else in the world.

Fossas in the Wild

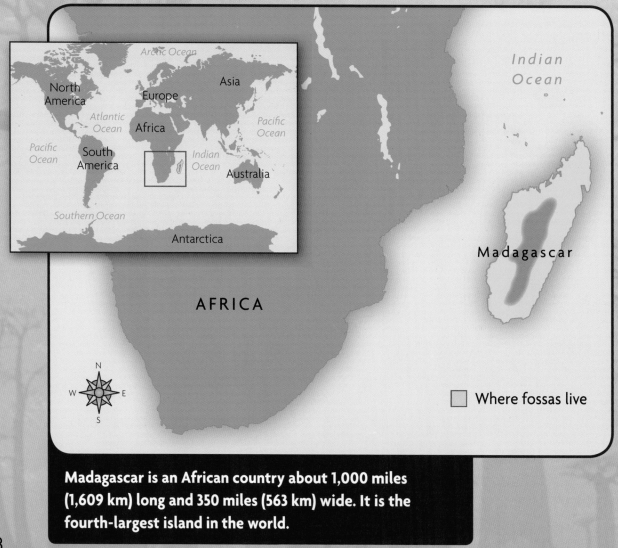

Where fossas live

Madagascar is an African country about 1,000 miles (1,609 km) long and 350 miles (563 km) wide. It is the fourth-largest island in the world.

Sadly, most of Madagascar's forests have been destroyed. Farmers have cut down and burned much of the island's trees in order to use the land to grow food. As a result, many rare **species** of plants have died out. Some of the animals that needed those plants for food and shelter are now **extinct**, too. Would Luke be able to study fossas under such difficult conditions?

About 90 percent of Madagascar's forests have been destroyed over the years.

Setting Up Camp

Luke set up two camps in Madagascar where he hoped to study fossas. One was in Ankarafantsika National Park. The other was in Kirindy Mitea National Park, which Luke described as "the middle of nowhere in the middle of nowhere." It had no roads, phones, or running water.

Luke (right) set up camps in forests crowded with trees and other plants.

Luke had to bring his own food, water, and gas to the camps. He also brought his own work equipment, including animal traps.

Catching a fossa would not be easy. Many people had lived in Madagascar for years without ever spotting one. "They are just so **elusive**," Luke explained. "They don't want to be seen."

Ankarafantsika National Park

Some parts of Madagascar have never been explored to this day.

Capturing a Fossa

Luke had a plan to catch a fossa. He knew that this rare creature is a meat-eater. So Luke and his team set out traps. They placed a live chicken in each one.

Luke set out cages like this one to catch a fossa.

In time, Luke managed to trap a fossa in a cage. After catching the animal, he shot the fossa with a dart to make it fall asleep. Luke was now finally able to safely study the animal up close.

A fossa trapped in a cage

It took about 90 seconds for the drug in Luke's dart to make the fossa fall asleep.

A Closer Look

Luke studied the fossa he captured. He saw that the animal looked like a long cat. It had sharp teeth and large feet with deadly claws.

A fossa in the wild

Fossas have very sharp teeth.

The fossa also had a very long tail. In fact, its tail was about as long as its body. In a tree, a fossa leaps from branch to branch like a squirrel. A fossa uses its long tail to keep its balance as it jumps through the air.

A fossa can move through the forest quickly and quietly.

For a long time, scientists thought that fossas were a type of **ancient** cat. Today, scientists have learned that fossas belong to the **mongoose** family.

A ring-tailed mongoose in Madagascar

Uncovering the Facts

As Luke began to study fossas, he learned many new things about this uncommon animal. Fossas are rarely seen during the day. So scientists had long believed that the animals hunt only at night. Luke discovered that this was not true. He saw fossas hunting during the day and at night.

A fossa has no set times for hunting, eating, or sleeping.

Scientists were also wrong about a fossa's **prey**. They had long thought that the animal hunts and kills only lemurs. Luke, however, found that a fossa eats any kind of animal it kills, from a mouse to a wild pig.

"It'll eat anything with a heartbeat," Luke said. "It's a killing machine."

A fossa will attack an animal that is as big as or even bigger than itself.

Luke got these scratches on his hands from a fossa he was studying.

Teamwork

Each year, Luke returned to Madagascar to do more fossa research. He became a college professor and took some of his students to the African island. He also worked with **volunteers** from an organization called the Earthwatch Institute. They wanted to help Luke collect **data** about the fossa.

Luke (back row, center) and his team with a fossa that they are studying

Luke and his team often traveled more than 12 miles (19 km) a day to track and trap a fossa.

In time, Luke and his **assistants** became experts at catching and studying fossas. They weighed and measured each fossa they caught. The team **analyzed** the animal's blood and health. Then they placed a radio collar on the fossa to track its movements after it was set free.

Luke used special tools to measure a fossa.

Fossas and Lemurs

Luke learned a great deal about the special **relationship** between fossas and lemurs. He found that fossas are the only kind of animal that can kill large lemurs in the wild. To stay safe, lemurs sleep in groups. Sometimes they crawl inside the hollow parts of trees to hide.

Lemurs hiding in a tree

Other lemurs stay safe by holding on to the ends of tree branches. If an enemy comes near, they can feel the **vibrations** the animal's movements make in the tree.

A fossa is still able to catch a lemur, however. This fierce hunter can race up a tree and grab a lemur so fast that its victim never knows what hit it.

A fossa attacks quickly. First it grabs its prey with its teeth. Then it rips open the victim's stomach with its sharp front claws.

A Delicate Balance

Fossas are a serious threat to lemurs. Yet Luke found that fossas are also an important part of Madagascar's **ecosystem**. Without them, other plants and animals in the forest might struggle to survive. Why?

Lemurs need to eat plants in order to survive.

Lemurs eat plants. Fossas then eat the lemurs. If there are not enough fossas, too many lemurs will survive. Over time, the lemurs will eat too many plants in the forest. Other animals that also need to eat those plants will **starve** to death. By hunting lemurs, fossas keep a healthy balance of plants and animals in the wild.

The fossa is the top predator in Madagascar. Other wild animals never attack it.

Spreading the Truth

Luke Dollar wanted the people of Madagascar to learn why fossas are so important to their country. Unfortunately, children there had always been taught that a fossa was like the big bad wolf. Scary bedtime stories told of fossas coming at night to steal babies from their cribs. "Be good, or the fossa will get you," parents warned.

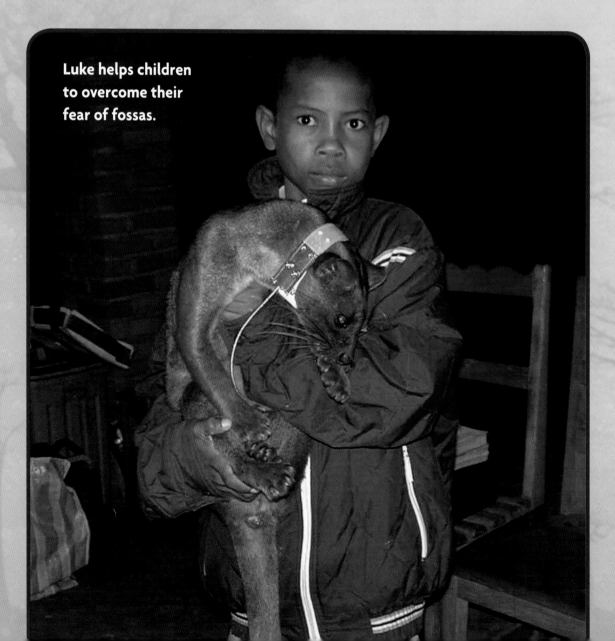

Luke helps children to overcome their fear of fossas.

Luke found that many farmers in Madagascar killed fossas whenever they got the chance. He told them, however, that they shouldn't kill fossas. These animals are actually helpful. They hunt and kill wild pigs and rats that would otherwise eat the farmers' rice crops. Luke passed out posters that read "Save the Fossa. Save the **Harvest**."

People in Madagascar often blamed fossas for the deaths of other animals, even when fossas did not kill them.

Today, fossas weigh between 11 and 22 pounds (5 and 10 kg). An early **ancestor** of the fossa was much bigger, weighing up to 200 pounds (91 kg).

The Future for Fossas

Luke Dollar has worked hard to spread the truth about fossas. Yet today, many people in Madagascar still kill them and destroy the forests where they live. As a result, the fossa is now an **endangered** animal. Luke estimates that as few as 2,500 now live in the wild.

Luke Dollar hopes to make people in Madagascar understand what fossas are really like.

Today, Luke looks for more ways to keep fossas safe. He is working to bring more **tourists** to Madagascar. The money visitors spend on their trips will hopefully help support villagers. Then they will not need to cut down trees in order to make money by farming. If Luke succeeds, fossas will finally have the bright future they deserve.

Tourists spend money that is badly needed by the poor people of Madagascar.

About 5,000 tourists visit Ankarafantsika National Park each year.

Fossa Facts

The fossa is a mammal. Like all mammals, a fossa is a **warm-blooded** animal that has a backbone, hair or fur on its skin, and drinks its mother's milk when it is a baby. Here are some other facts about this uncommon animal.

Weight	**males:** 13–22 pounds (6–10 kg) **females:** 11–15 pounds (5–7 kg)
Length	**males:** 29–31 inches (74–79 cm) long, plus a tail that is 27–35 inches (69–89 cm) long **females:** 25–27 inches (64–69 cm) long, plus a tail that is the same size
Food	lemurs, mice, snakes, chickens, wild pigs, fish
Life Span	15–20 years
Habitat	the forests of Madagascar
Population	about 2,500 in the wild

More Uncommon Animals

The fossa is one kind of uncommon animal in Madagascar. Many other unusual animals also live there.

Aye-Aye

- The aye-aye is a rare kind of lemur that lives only in the trees of Madagascar.
- The exact number of aye-ayes that live in the wild is not known.
- They are an endangered animal and protected by law.
- Aye-ayes eat insects, fruit, nuts, and seeds.
- Many people in Madagascar kill aye-ayes because they believe that seeing one will bring death or bad luck.
- Aye-ayes sleep during the day and are active at night.

Madagascar Hissing Cockroach

- The Madagascar hissing cockroach got its name from the sound it makes when it feels threatened.
- These roaches are about two to three inches (5 to 7.6 cm) long.
- They do not live in people's homes. Instead, they live on the ground in forests, usually in logs and fallen leaves.
- They are most active at night when they are looking for food, such as rotting plants, dead animals, and fruit.
- Madagascar hissing cockroaches live for two to five years.

Glossary

analyzed (AN-uh-lyzed) studied carefully

ancestor (AN-sess-tur) a family member who lived a long time ago

ancient (AYN-shunt) very old

assistants (uh-SISS-tuhnts) people who help someone do a job

data (DAY-tuh) information often in the form of numbers

ecosystem (EE-koh-*siss*-tuhm) a community of animals and plants that depend on one another to live

elusive (ih-LOO-siv) very hard to catch or find

endangered (en-DAYN-jurd) in danger of dying out

extinct (ek-STINGKT) when a kind of plant or animal has died out; no more of its kind is living anywhere in the world

harvest (HAR-vist) the gathering of crops that are ready to be eaten

island (EYE-luhnd) a piece of land surrounded by water on all sides

lemurs (LEE-murz) furry animals that usually have long tails and large eyes; they are in the primate family and live mainly in Madagascar

mongoose (MON-gooss) an animal that lives in Africa and Asia and has a slim body, a long tail, and usually brown or gray fur; it is known for its skill at killing cobras and other poisonous snakes

predator (PRED-uh-tur) an animal that hunts other animals for food

prey (PRAY) an animal that is hunted and eaten by another animal

radio collars (RAY-dee-oh KOL-urz) collars that send out radio signals and are put on animals so that their movements can be tracked

rare (RAIR) not often found or seen

relationship (ri-LAY-shuhn-ship) the way in which things are connected

species (SPEE-sheez) groups that animals or plants are divided into according to similar characteristics; members of the same animal species can have offspring together

starve (STARV) to die from lack of food

tourists (TOOR-ists) people who travel and visit places for fun

vibrations (vye-BRAY-shunz) quick back-and-forth shaking movements that can be felt

vicious (VISH-uhss) violent and dangerous

volunteers (*vol*-uhn-TIHRZ) people who offer to do a job for no pay

warm-blooded (*worm*-BLUHD-id) having a body that almost always stays the same temperature no matter the temperature of the environment

Bibliography

Croke, Vicki. "The Deadliest Carnivore," *Discover Magazine* (April 1, 2000).
discovermagazine.com/2000/apr/featdeadliest

Harris, Margaret L. "Living a Double Life," *Dukenvironment Magazine* (Spring 2003).
nicholas.duke.edu/dukenvironment/sp03/action.html

Pickrell, John. "Tracking the Fossa, Africa's Elusive Island Predator," *National Geographic* (January 18, 2005).
news.nationalgeographic.com/news/2004/06/0602_040602_fossa.html

Tennesen, Michael. "The Fossa and the Lemur," *National Wildlife Magazine* (April/May 2006).
www.nationalwildlifefederation.org/nationalwildlife
/article.cfm?issueID=104&articleID=1317

Tyson, Peter. "Fossa!," NOVA *Online Adventure* (May 25, 2000).
www.pbs.org/wgbh/nova/madagascar/dispatches/20000525.html

Read More

Blauer, Ettagale, and Jason Lauré. *Madagascar (Enchantment of the World)*. New York: Children's Press (2000).

Corwin, Jeff. *Into Wild Madagascar*. San Diego, CA: Blackbirch Press (2004).

Lasky, Kathryn. *Shadows in the Dawn: The Lemurs of Madagascar*. San Diego, CA: Harcourt (1998).

Oluonye, Mary N. *Madagascar*. Minneapolis, MN: Carolrhoda Books (2000).

Learn More Online

To learn more about fossas, visit
www.bearportpublishing.com/UncommonAnimals

Index

About the Author

Meish Goldish has written more than 100 books for children. His book *Fossil Tales* won the Learning Magazine Teachers' Choice Award.